Bilingual Edition

READING POWER

Edición Bilingüe

THE CHEETAH

World's Fastest Land Animal

El guepardo

El animal terrestre más veloz del mundo

Joy Paige

The Rosen Publishing Group's

PowerKids Press™ & Buenas Letras™

New York

1

Published in 2003 by The Rosen Publishing Group, Inc.
29 East 21st Street, New York, NY 10010
Copyright © 2003 by The Rosen Publishing Group, Inc.

First Bilingual Edition 2003
First Edition in English 2002

Book Design: Michael DeLisio
Photo Credits: Cover, pp. 5, 6–7, 9 © Photo Safari/Digital Vision; pp. 10–11, 12–13, 20–21 © Animals in Action/Digital Stock; pp. 14–15, 19 © Corbis; p. 17 © Animals Animals

Paige, Joy
The Cheetah: World's fastest mammal/El guepardo: El animal terrestre más veloz del mundo/Joy Paige ; traducción al español: Spanish Educational Publishing
p. cm. — (Record-Breaking Animals)
Includes bibliographical references and index.
ISBN 0-8239-6892-8 (lib. bdg.)
1. Cheetah—Juvenile literature. [1. Cheetah. 2. Spanish Language Materials—Bilingual.] I. Title.

Printed in The United States of America

Contents

Contenido

A cheetah is a big cat.

Los guepardos son felinos.

5

Cheetahs live in Africa.
Cheetahs also live in Asia.

Los guepardos viven en África.
También hay guepardos
en Asia.

Asia

Africa/África

7

Cheetahs live in the open.
They live in grasslands.

Los guepardos viven
en lugares abiertos.
Viven en las praderas.

Cheetahs run fast. They can run up to 70 miles (112km) an hour.

Los guepardos corren muy rápido.
Pueden correr a
70 millas (112km) por hora.

Cheetahs have long legs.
Long legs help cheetahs take
big steps.

Los guepardos tienen
las patas muy largas.
Dan pasos muy grandes.

Cheetahs have long, flat tails.
Their tails help them keep their
balance when they run fast.

Los guepardos tienen la cola
larga y aplanada.
La cola los ayuda a mantener
el equilibrio cuando corren.

Cheetahs have short claws.
Short claws grip the ground.
This helps cheetahs run fast.

Los guepardos tienen
las garras cortas.
Clavan las garras en el suelo
para correr más rápido.

17

Cheetahs run fast to catch other animals. Cheetahs then eat the animals they catch.

Los guepardos corren rápido para cazar otros animales. Los guepardos comen los animales que cazan.

Cheetahs are the fastest
animals on land.

Los guepardos son los animales
terrestres más veloces.

Glossary

Africa (**af**-ruh-kuh) the second-largest continent in the world

Asia (**ay**-zhuh) the largest continent in the world

balance (**bal**-uhns) keeping steady

claws (**klawz**) nails attached to an animal's foot

grasslands (**gras**-landz) land with grass on it

Glosario

África El continente más grande del mundo después de Asia

Asia El continente más grande del mundo

equilibrio (el) posición normal

felino (el) grupo de mamíferos al que pertenecen el gato, el leopardo y la pantera

garras (las) uñas puntiagudas

pradera (la) terreno plano cubierto de hierba

Resources / Recursos

Here are more books to read about the cheetah:
Otros libros que puedes leer sobre el guepardo:

Big Cats
by Bobbie Kalman and Tammy Everts
Crabtree Publishing (1994)

Cheetah
by Taylor Morrison
Henry Holt & Company (1998)

Web sites
Due to the changing nature of Internet links, PowerKids Press
has developed an online list of Web sites related to the subject
of this book. This site is updated regularly. Please use this link to
access the list:

Sitios web
Debido a las constantes modificaciones en los sitios de Internet,
PowerKids Press ha desarrollado una guía on-line de sitios
relacionados al tema de este libro. Nuestro sitio web se
actualiza constantemente. Por favor utiliza la siguiente dirección
para consultar la lista:

http://www.buenasletraslinks.com/chl/tmb

Word count in English: 98
Número de palabras en español: 104

Index

Índice